RUNYANKORE/RUKIGA-
ENGLISH PICTURE DICTIONARY

Over 1000 new words, songs, rhymes from Western Uganda

Mother Tongue Series

DR. MOLLYNN MUGISHA-OTIM

AuthorHouse™ UK
1663 Liberty Drive
Bloomington, IN 47403 USA
www.authorhouse.co.uk
UK TFN: 0800 0148641 (Toll Free inside the UK)
UK Local: 02036 956322 (+44 20 3695 6322 from outside the UK)

ISBN: 978-1-6655-9731-9 (sc)
ISBN: 978-1-6655-9730-2 (e)

Print information available on the last page.

Published by AuthorHouse 04/13/2022

authorHOUSE®

RUNYANKORE/RUKIGA-
ENGLISH PICTURE DICTIONARY

Over 1000 new words, songs, rhymes from Western Uganda

Dedication

This book is dedicated to children from Western Uganda living in the diaspora, their parents and all those making effort to keep their connection with their culture through learning the Runyakitara languages.

Acknowledgements

Special thanks to all members of the greater Kashesya family. Thank you for your help as we reminisced about our childhood memories, the games we played and songs we sang so naturally. Without you filling in the gaps where my memory could not, this book would not have been completed easily. Special thanks to my dear Aunt Jeninah Tumwesigye who took time to proof read the manuscript of this book.

Huge thanks also goes to Robbie Zein, my special soul sister from another mother. Your unconditional love and support is what anyone needs from a friend in this world and forever.

Finally, I thank my husband, Stephen and children Myrhon and Kayla, who not only give me space to fit writing in our busy family schedule, but also always there to listen and encourage me to write more books to promote our cultures.

INTRODUCTION

Runyankore is a Bantu language spoken by around two and a half million people in south-west Uganda. The language is also known as Nyankore, Nyankole, Nkole, Orunyankore and Orunyankole. Runyankore is mainly spoken in the Mbarara, Bushenyi, Ntungamo, Kiruhura, Ibanda, Isingiro, Rukungiri and parts of Kitagwenda districts.

Rukiga, also known as Kiga language is a similar and partially mutually intelligible with the Runyankore langauage. It is largely spoken in the ancient Kigezi region which includes about 5 districts, namely; Rubanda, Rukiga, Kabale, Kanungu and some parts of Rukungiri. Kiga is spoken natively by about 1.3 million people in Uganda.

Some people argue that because it is so similar to Runyankore, they consider them dialects of the same language, hence the term Runyankore-Rukiga.

Whilst a very old language, the written literature is still not common place. There are very few (illustrated) children's books for young ones to learn the language. That is why I have created this simple illustrated book.

When learning Runyankore-Rukiga, it is important to remember the following:

➢ Runyankore and Rukiga are generally spoken very quickly
➢ There is Variation in pronunciation and spelling based on region
➢ The letters "R" and "L" are interchangeable, there is little use of the letter "L" and more use of "R"
➢ R's are rolled
➢ C is generally pronounced as ch and ki as ky. There are many "ch" sounds (written as 'ki' and 'ky'). So ekicuncu would be pronounced as ekyi-chu-nchu;
➢ There are often half a dozen ways of saying the same thing!

This book aims to help you pick up essentials of the language to be able to make some comfortable introductions and simple conversations. To become affluent will take longer practice and dedication. I hope this book will help stimulate parents to use the language daily with their children from an early age.

Because Runyankore is a Bantu language, there is dialect continua as can be expected. People from Mbarara, Bushenyi speak Runyankore, while people from Fort Portal in Tooro Kingdom speak Rutooro. It is common that areas in between these two speak a dialect that is intermediate between Runyankore and Rutooro. Likewise, the people in Kabale speak Rukiiga, and people between Kabale and Bushenyi speak a dialect that is intermediate between Runyankore and Rukiga. The four languages (Rutooro, Rukiga, Runyankore and Runyoro) are so close that a standardized version of these is called "**Runyakitara**"

Other languages closely related to Runyakitara

People from Northern Tanzania bordering Uganda speak similar a language (Haya) to Runyakitara. Also closely related are the **Nyambo**, or **Ragwe** in Tanzania. They speak a language called **Kinyambo**. They are a Bantu ethnic and linguistic group based in the Karagwe District of Kagera Region in far northwestern Tanzania. The Nyambo population is estimated to number 670,000. Their closest relatives are the Haya people.

The **Haya** (or **Bahaya**) are a Bantu ethnic group based in Kagera Region, northwestern Tanzania, on the western side of Lake Victoria. With over one million people, it is estimated the Haya make up approximately 2% of the population of Tanzania. Their language is **Ruhaya** or **Kihaya**.

Also closely related are the **Bahema**, or **Hema**. They speak **Kihema**, also sometimes known as Southern Hema. It is a Bantu language and is one of three languages spoken by the Hema people of the Democratic Republic of the Congo. Their population is estimated to be 160,000 and they live mainly in Ituri Province in the Democratic Republic of the Congo.

This is a map of east Africa showing areas where Runyakitara speaking people are indigenous in Uganda; the Bahaya and the Nyambo in Tanzania; and the Hema in Congo

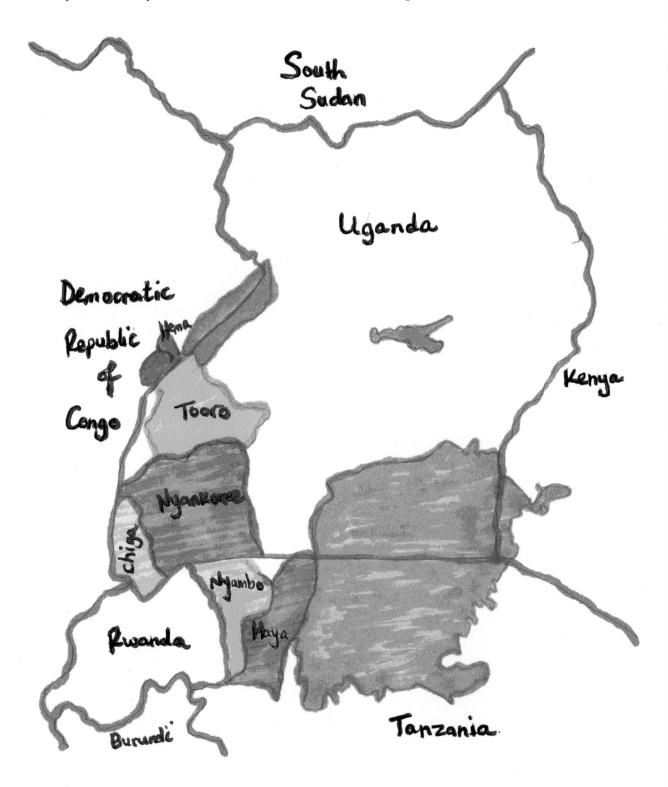

Play and learn
Okuzana n'okwega

Enyuguta
Letters

Eshuura
Numbers

Ekaraamu
Pencils

Akachumu
Pen

Ekitabo
Book

Orubaaho
(Black) Board

Omupiira
Ball

Omupiira
Ball

Cooka
Chalk

Entebbe
Chair

Emeeza
Table

Omuguha
Skipping Rope

Erangi
Colours

Ekishaahi
Playground

Omupira guri aha'meeza

The ball is on the table

Omuhinganzima/ omwanganzima gwine erangi mushanju

A rainbow has 7 colours

Omushomesa nahandika enyuguta n'eshuura aha rubaaho

The teacher writes letters and numbers on the board

Ninzana omu kishaahi buri eizoba

I play in the playground daily/everyday

Ebendera ya Uganda eyine amabara ashaatu: kiraguju, kinnekye/kihongwa na kitukura

The Uganda flag has three colours: black, yellow and red

Enyaruju nehindura amabara gaayo

A chameleon changes its colours

Embeba eri ahansi y'entebbe

The rat is under the chair

Tebekanisa emeeza turye

Prepare the table and we eat

Maama nanshomera ekitaabo buri kiro ntakabyamire

My mummy reads a book to me every night before bed

Ninkunda kweega okubara na orujungu ah'ishomero

I like learning mathematics and English at school

Counting - Okubara

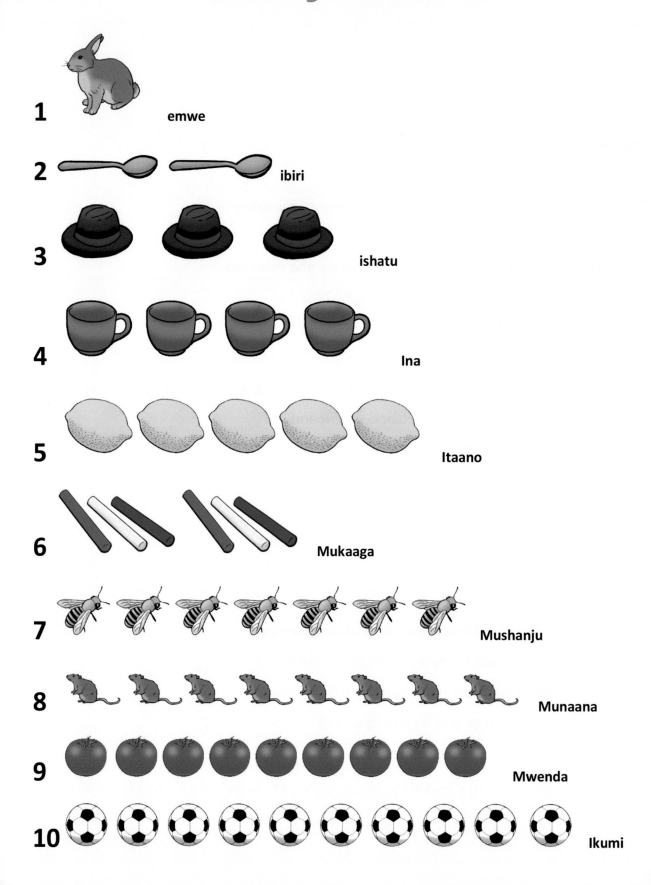

1 emwe

2 ibiri

3 ishatu

4 Ina

5 Itaano

6 Mukaaga

7 Mushanju

8 Munaana

9 Mwenda

10 Ikumi

11 Ikumi nemwe

12 Ikumi nibiri

13 Ikumi nishatu

14 Ikumi nina

15 Ikumi nitaano

16 Ikumi namukaaga

17 Ikumi namushanju

18 Ikumi namunaana

19 Ikumi namwenda

20 Makumi abiri

21 Abiri nemwe

30 Makumi ashatu

31 Ashatu nemwe

40 Makumi ana / makumiana/makumyana

41 Makumiana nemwe

50. makumi ataano

51. ataano nemwe

60. nkaaga

61. nkaaga nemwe

70 Nshanju

71 Nshanju nemwe

80 Kinaana

81 Kinaana nemwe

90 Kyenda

91 Kyenda nemwe

100 Igana (Kikumi)

101 Igana emwe

150 Igana ataano

200 Bibiri

300 Bishatu

400 Bina

500 Bitaano

600 Rukaga

700 rushanju

800 Runana

900 Rwenda

1,000 Rukumi

1500 Rukimi nabitaano

2,000 Ekumibiri

10,000 Omutwaro

20,000 Emitwaro ebiri

100,000 Emitwaro Ikumi

1,000,000 Akahumbi

Obukoni

Sticks

Abashaija bashatu

Bine obukoni

Obukoni nkobwe wabuterana

Emwe ibiri ishatu ina itao

Mukaga mushanju munana Mwenda ikumi

1234 nkabasirikare

Three men have sticks

The sticks can be combined

One two three four five

Six seven eight nine ten

1234 like soldiers

Abantu
People

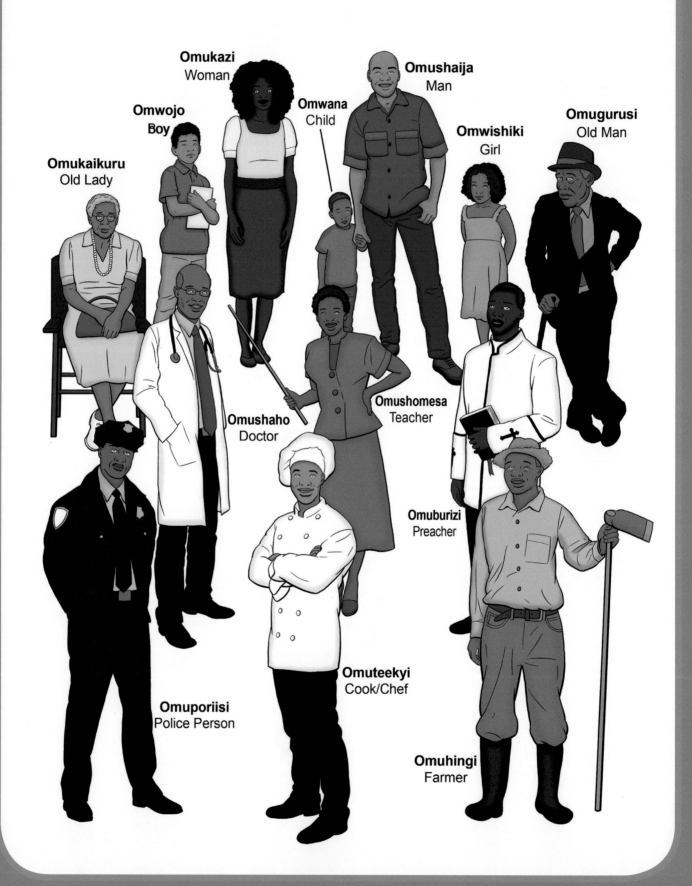

Omukazi Woman

Omwojo Boy

Omwana Child

Omushaija Man

Omwishiki Girl

Omugurusi Old Man

Omukaikuru Old Lady

Omushaho Doctor

Omushomesa Teacher

Omuburizi Preacher

Omuporiisi Police Person

Omuteekyi Cook/Chef

Omuhingi Farmer

Tata wangye ni omushaho kandi mama wangye ni omushomesa

My Father is a doctor and my mother is a teacher

Eka yeitu arimu abantu bana: tata, mama, munyanyazi, na nyowe

Our home is made up of 4 people: daddy, mummy, my brother and myself

Omubuurizi nashabira abantu omu kaniisa/kereziya

The priest prays for people in church

Tindikutiina aba polisi

I am not afraid of the police

Swhenkuru ni omugurusi. Nyakwenkuru ni omukaikuru

Grandpa is an old man. Grandma is an old woman

Za hoteeri ziine abateeki barungi

Hotels have good chefs

Abashomesa baine omugasho gwamani om'eihanga

Teachers are very useful for the country

Abahingi nibakoora n'amani munonga

Farmers work very hard.

Abaana nibetaaga kuzana aheeru buri izooba

Children need to play outside everyday

Abaana bato nibatiina ebikatu

Young children fear injections

Abana baine kuyamba abantu abakuru

Children should help older people

Nabugana Akakaikuru

I met an old lady

Nabugana akakaikuru, otyo eee

Kekoraire embeba eibiri, otyo eee

Nakateera entomi eibiri, otyo eee

Kagwa namaizi kaarira, otyo eee

Nagwa nesheko nasheka, otyo eee

Ebijuma

Fruits

Omuyembe
Mango

Omucungwa
Orange

Enanaasi
Pineaple

Endimu
Lemon

Mangada
Tangerine

Eipapaari
Pawpaw

Obutunda
Passion Fruits

Vakedo
Ovaccado

Amapeera
Guavas

Ekifenensi/Fene
Jack Fruit

Eminekye
Yellow Bananas

Emizaabibu
Grapes

Amatehe
Heaven Fruits

Shwento/ Nyokoromi wangye nakunda kurya amapapari omukasheshe

My (paternal/maternal) uncle likes to eat pawpaws in the morning

Nitukora obubanda omuri esaano ya muhogo n'eminekye ya kabaragara

We make pancakes from cassava flour and yellow bananas

Omuntu omugimu naarya ebijuma némboga buri eizooba

A healthy person eats fruits and vegetables every day.

Endimu nizisharira

Lemons are sour

Otatekamu sukari! Omunanaasi nigunuririra

Don't put in sugar. Pineapple juice is very sweet

Ninkozesa ebijuma kokora Omwegonozo

I use fruits to make a dessert

Ninkozesa ebijuma kukora omwegonozo

I like yellow guavas

Omuti gwa fene gugumire okutemba

A fene tree is hard to climb

Fene enuzire kwonka nenuuka munonga

Fene tastes good but has a strong small

Katungurucumu nenuuka munonga

Garlic has a strong smell

This is the song we used to sing when we are going into the thick swampy woods to get amatehe fruits. Because these woods had many snakes which also liked to eat the same fruits, we would sing this song to the snake to say please come out so we can come in. We promised the snake that we would eat the unripe (black fruits) and leave for him the ripe (red ones)

The song gave us courage to go in and I guess warned the snakes that we were nearby 😊

Shwenkuru

Shwenkuru rugamu nzemu

Nabaana baawe barugemu

Kubararugemu naanye ninzamu

Ninyihamu agari kwiragura

Nindekamu agarikutukura

> Grandpa come out and I come in
>
> Tell your children too to come out
>
> When they are out I will come in
>
> I promise to take out the black(unripe) fruits
>
> And I will leave the (red) ripe ones for you

Emboga
Vegetables

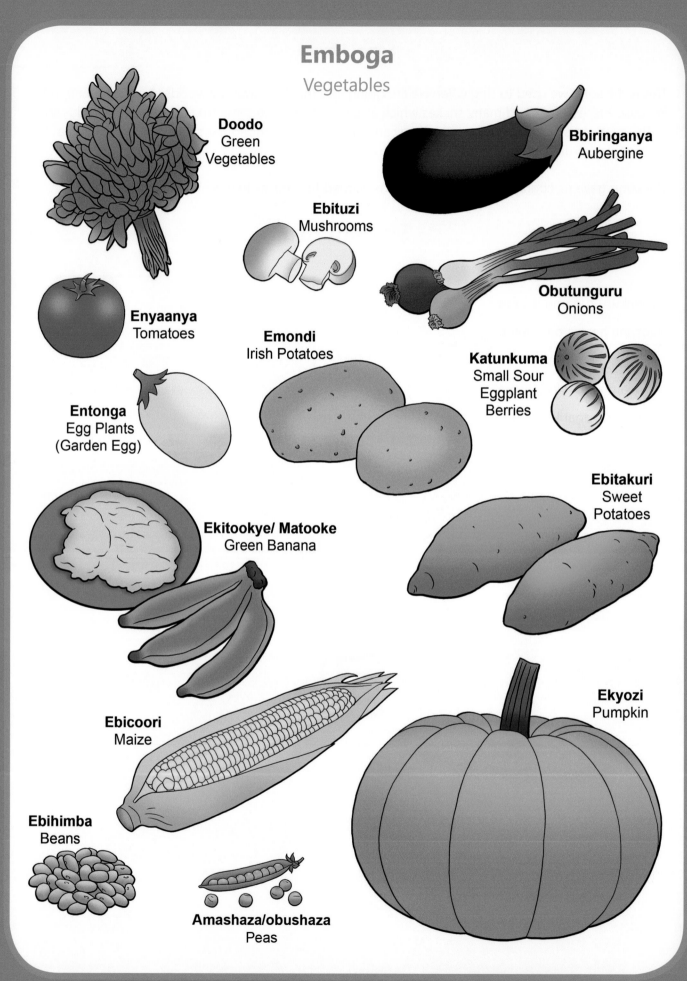

Doodo
Green Vegetables

Bbiringanya
Aubergine

Ebituzi
Mushrooms

Obutunguru
Onions

Enyaanya
Tomatoes

Emondi
Irish Potatoes

Katunkuma
Small Sour Eggplant Berries

Entonga
Egg Plants (Garden Egg)

Ebitakuri
Sweet Potatoes

Ekitookye/ Matooke
Green Banana

Ekyozi
Pumpkin

Ebicoori
Maize

Ebihimba
Beans

Amashaza/obushaza
Peas

Ninkunda kurya ebitakuri n'emboga zébinyeebwa

I like to eat sweet potatoes and groundnuts sauce

Chipus na krisipus nibazisiika okuruga omu emondi

Chips and Crisps are fried from Irish potatoes

Shwenkazi ni omushoromerezi

My aunt works as a vegetable picker in the farm

Amaisho gangye nigarira naba ninshashara obutunguru

My eyes cry when I am cutting onions

Ebinyabwooya nibikura biba ebihuguhugu

Caterpillars grow into butterflies

Amashaza amabisi ni ga kijubwe

Raw peas are green

Nywa supu y'ebyoozi harimu karoti

Drink pumpkin soup with carrots

Abantu ba BuDutchi nibakunda kurya supu ya obushaza omu mbeho

Dutch people like to eat pea soup in winter

Katunkuma nesharira

Katunkuma tastes bitter

Kosiyo

This song reminds children of the dangers of not listening to adults' advice

Kosiya akaba arimuto

akaba arimuto, akaba arimuto

Nyina we yamugambira

Yamugambira, yamugambira

Ngu otaza omukibira

Omukibira, omukibira

Kosiyo yayanga yazayo

yayanga yazayo, yayanga yazayo

Akati kamuchumita

Kamuchumita kamuchumita

Kosiyo yija narira

yija narira yija narira

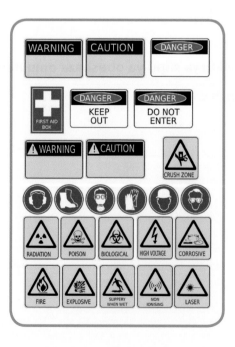

Ebyokurisa
Eating utensils

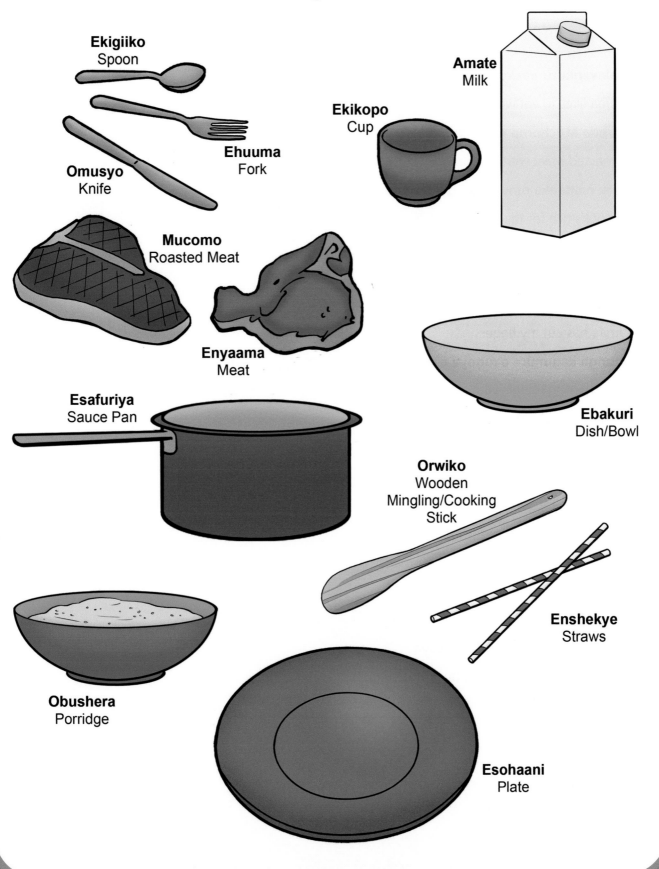

Ekigiiko
Spoon

Ehuuma
Fork

Omusyo
Knife

Ekikopo
Cup

Amate
Milk

Mucomo
Roasted Meat

Enyaama
Meat

Esafuriya
Sauce Pan

Ebakuri
Dish/Bowl

Orwiko
Wooden
Mingling/Cooking
Stick

Enshekye
Straws

Obushera
Porridge

Esohaani
Plate

Nywakwenkuru naakunda kuriisa engaro ze

Grandma likes to eat with her hands

Ninkunda Muchomo na Kachumbari

I like roasted meat with kachumbari

Maama naateeka omucheeri gw'esande yoona omu safuriya empango

Mum cooks rice for the whole week in a big saucepan

Obukopo bwa kaawa ni bukye munonga

Coffee cups are very small

Omusyo gwashara orukumu rwangye

The knife has cut my finger

Akahunga kagumire okugoya n'orwiko

Posho is hard to mingle with a mingling stick

Taata nanywa obushera aha kyantsya

Daddy takes porridge for breakfast

Ninyenda kurya pilau erimu enyama y'ente

I would like to eat pilau with beef

Enshekye z'ebipapura ni nungi ahansi yaitu

Paper straws are good for our environment

Amate g'embuzi gagumire kubona

Goat milk is hard to find

Otakwataho! obushera nibukwosya

Don't touch! The porridge will burn you

Naga kasasiro aheeru

Throw away the rubbish outside

Song (Lullaby): Oyonkye nkusherekye

Chorus

Oyonkye nkushereke iwe kaana kangye
Oyonke Nkusherekye kanywa mushwaga
Kundiba nafiire iwe kaana kangye
Orye obunyansi nk'ente iwe kaana Kangye

Kundiba nafiire iwe kaana kangye
Oyambukye orusharara iwe kaana kangye
Ogyende owa nyakwento iwe kaana kangye
Oyonkye nkushereke iwe kaana kangye

Ndosire omuhiigo guribukanga
Nibenda kukwita iwe mwana wangye
Ekikooni kyomuhigi kicwa omugongo
Ekyo kibwa rukamba kinuukanuuka

Kundiba nafiire iwe kaana kangye
Orye obunyansi nk'ente iwe kashugira ngoma
Orengyeseho otwizi kaserebembe
Nibyo byorufuzi kashugira ngoma

Omunju
Household

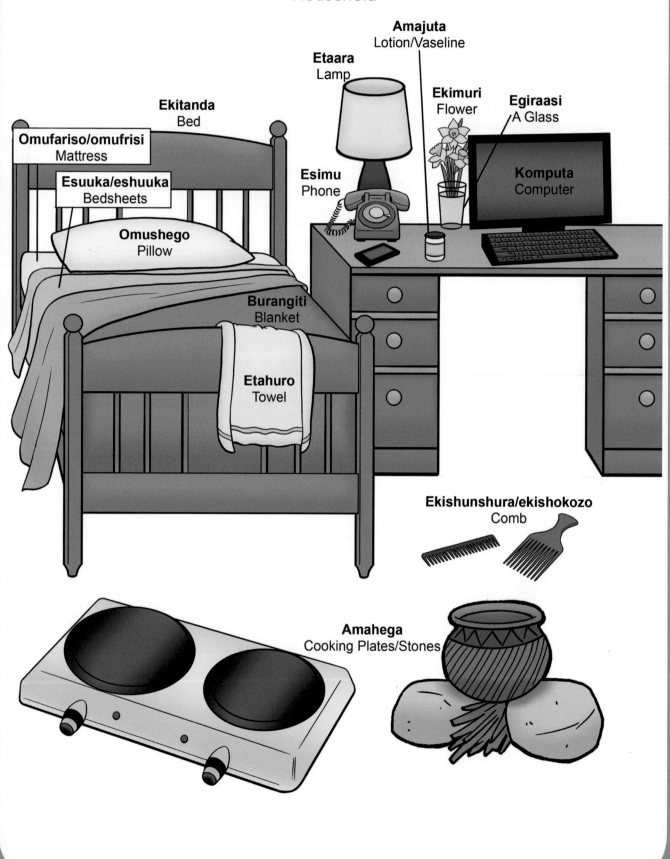

Ekitanda
Bed

Omufariso/omufrisi
Mattress

Esuuka/eshuuka
Bedsheets

Omushego
Pillow

Burangiti
Blanket

Etahuro
Towel

Etaara
Lamp

Amajuta
Lotion/Vaseline

Esimu
Phone

Ekimuri
Flower

Egiraasi
A Glass

Komputa
Computer

Ekishunshura/ekishokozo
Comb

Amahega
Cooking Plates/Stones

Nimbyama hariho etaara

I sleep with the lamp on

Ninkozesa omushego ogworobi

I use a soft pillow

Shitama aha meeza turye

Sit on the table and we eat

Omuri Uganda, nimbyama n'esuuka yonka ahabwokuba ekibiga/ekyoya nikingi

In Uganda, I sleep with only bedsheets because its hot

Enkaito/ engaito zangye ziri ahansi y'ekitanda

My shoes are under the bed

Nyabura yara ekitanda kyawe buri kasheshe

Please make your bed every morning

Ebimuri byiine erangi nyingi

Flowers are colourful

Ninyikirizibwa eshaha emwe omwizooba aha komputa

I am allowed one hour a day on the computer

Nimanya enamba y'esimu y'abazeire bangye

I know my parents phone number

Hanika etahuro waaheza kunaaba ebaase kwoma gye

Hang the towel to dry well after bathing

Amajuta ga shea butter gabonaire

Shea butter cream is nice

Ninyoza esuuka zangye buri rwamukaaga

I wash my bedsheets every Saturday

Enju yaitu eyine amatembezo/amadaara maingi

Our house has many stairs

Temba amadaara

Climb the ladder

Rhyme of sequencing

Natema akati karara

I cut a little stick and it escaped

Nateema akati Kaarara

Kaarara nikaza Igara

Igaara owa Ntambiko

Ntambiko yampa ekisyo

Ekisyo Naakiha abagyesi

Abagyesi bampa oburo

Oburo naabuha warukoko

Warukoko yampa eihuri

Eihuri naariha omukama

Omukama yampa ente

Ente naagishweza Omukazi

Omukazi yanzaarira omwana

Omwana namweta Mugarura

Agume agarure abya owaishe neby'owaishenkuru

I cut a little stick and it escaped

It escaped going towards Igara

Igara where Ntambiko lives

Ntabiko gave me a knife

I gave the knife to the millet harvesters

The harvesters gave me millet

I gave the millet to the chicken

The chicken gave me an egg

I gave the egg to the king

The king gave me a cow

I used the cow to marry a wife

The wife gave me a son

I called the son Mugarura (the one who returns what is lost)

He always returns what belongs to his father and grandfather

Amatungo
Domestic animals

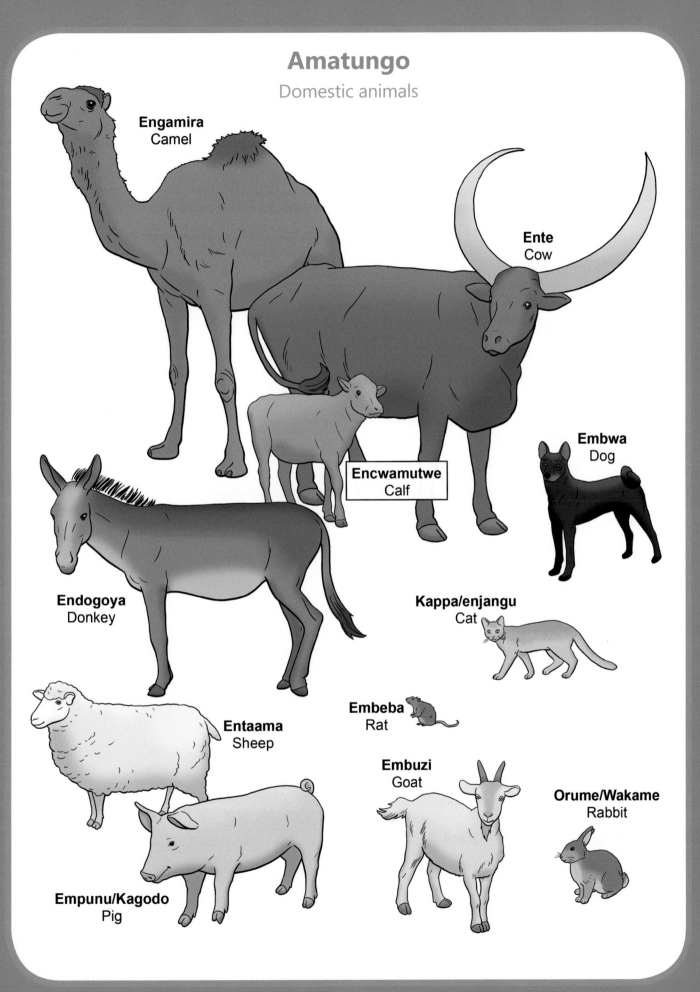

Engamira
Camel

Ente
Cow

Embwa
Dog

Encwamutwe
Calf

Endogoya
Donkey

Kappa/enjangu
Cat

Entaama
Sheep

Embeba
Rat

Embuzi
Goat

Orume/Wakame
Rabbit

Empunu/Kagodo
Pig

Embwa yaitu nibagyeta Rukamba

Our dog is called Rukamba

Twine ente Mushanju. Amaziina gaazo ni: rugaaju, kasiina, kyozi, bihogo, kyasha na shamaitu

We have 7 cows. They are called: rugaaju, kasiina, kyozi, nyonga, bihogo, kyasha and shamaitu

Embeba nizitiina Kappa

Rats are afraid of cats

Ente yaitu ezaire encwamutwe ibiri

Our cow gave birth to 2 calves

Ente za Nkore ziine amahembe maraingwa gagondami

Ankole cows have long curved horns

Gaaju eine encwamutwe y'omwezi gumwe

The brown cow has a 1-month-old calf

Omuriisa naakira kutwarira enyamaishwa ze ebishushsu by'ebitokye

The animal keeper normally takes banana peels for his animals

Entaama ziriire ebihimba bya swenkazi omu musiri

Sheep ate my auntie's beans in the garden

Obume nibushaagura/ nibuzaara abaana baingi

Rabbits produce many babies

Shwenkuru naatunga empunu n'embuzi

Grandpa rears pigs and goats

Omubaagi naayenda ebinyamaiswa ebihango byonka

The butcher wants big animals only

Tinkanywaga amate g'engamira

I have never drunk camel milk

Embeba eyesherekire ahansi y'entebe

The rat is hiding under the couch/chair

Mpa Enkoni

Give me a stick

Mp'enkoni, mp'enkoni, mp'enkoni

Mpa enkoni engarama zaijire

Zaijire nizicunda ebinwa

Ebinwa bya Rwakitendegyere

Rwakitendegyere enkuba emuteere

Emuteerere ahaiguru mpariya

Mpariya hariho obwitiro

Obwitiro buzarwa n'enkura

Enkura eshoroma eteekire

Eteekire akaro n'emboga

Emboga zitarimu omwonyo

Omwonyo guruga Isharara

Isharara omunda yengoma

Y'engoma, y'engoma, y'engoma

Ebikooko Eby'omwishwa

Animals in the wild

Enkyende
Monkey

Enjojo
Elephant

Embarasi
Horse

Empundu
Gorrilla

Ekicuncu
Lion

Embogo
Buffallo

Akanyankogote
Tortoise

Gonya
Crocodile

Enjoka
Snake

Ekyenyanja
Fish

Ekikyere
Frog

Mushushu
Shrew

Ekinyantida
Snail

Gonya neetuura omu mugyera

A Crocodile lives in a river

Empuuta n'ekyenyanja kihango

Nile perch is a very big fish

Akanyankogote nikabaasa kuhangaara emyaka igana

A tortoise can live for 100 years

Ninzaana omuzaano gwa "guruka makyere"

I am playing the game of "jump like a frog"

Engagi/ Empundu nizituura hamwe omu makumi

Gorillas live together in groups

Enjoka ezimwe tiziine butwa

Some snakes don't have poison

Enjojo n'enyamaishwa mpango munonga

Elephants are very big animals

Embogo nebaasa kurwanisa ekicuncu

A buffalo can fight off a lion

Embeba eburiire omu mwina omukishengye/ omukidongo/ omukisiika

The mouse disappeared into a hole in the wall.

Ekicuncu n'omugabe w'ebinyamaishwa byoona

The lion is the king of the jungle

Game: Meketa

Meketa is a Luganda word which means to eat. This is a game we used to play to test memory, concentration and steadiness concerning the foods that can be eaten and not eaten. It was also played in groups from 5 up to even 20 people with one leader who would also be in charge of spotting and eliminating those who make a mistake by mentioning what is not right.

The leader sings these two words, *Meki meki* and the other members reply *meketa*. Then he/she mentions an animal and if the animal or bird is edible all the members are expected to say ***meketa***.If it is not edible, they are expected to say NO NO. Members must not think so hard, hesitate or stay silent. If they do, then they also fail just like a person who said a wrong answer. If a member does or replies the opposite, then the leader with the help of other members spot him/her out and they are eliminated. The game continues until only one person remains who is regarded as winner of the game. The winner becomes the leader and the game is started again with all the members rejoining.

Leader: Meki meki,

Others; Meketa

Leader: Nyama y'ente (beef).

Others: meketa (because cow's beef is edible.) If someone hesitates or says no no is out

Leader: Nyama y'embwa (dog's meat)

Others: No No

Whoever hesitates, or says meketa or stays silent is out

Other possible animals/birds:

Nyama.. y'embuzi; mbogo; entama; empundu; kanyankogote; enkoko; enjoka....

INSECTS
Obukooko

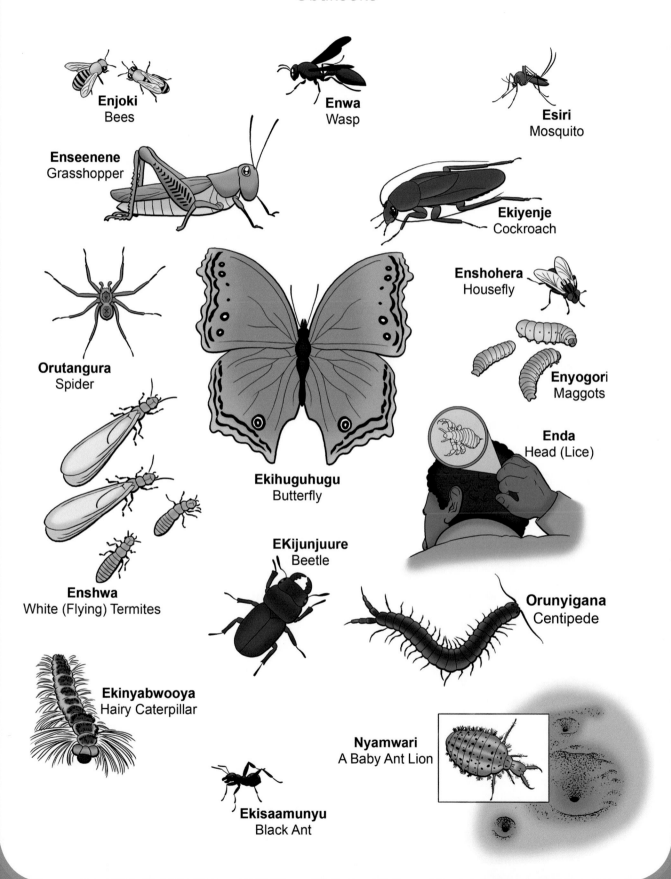

Enjoki
Bees

Enwa
Wasp

Esiri
Mosquito

Enseenene
Grasshopper

Ekiyenje
Cockroach

Enshohera
Housefly

Orutangura
Spider

Enyogori
Maggots

Ekihuguhugu
Butterfly

Enda
Head (Lice)

Enshwa
White (Flying) Termites

EKijunjuure
Beetle

Orunyigana
Centipede

Ekinyabwooya
Hairy Caterpillar

Nyamwari
A Baby Ant Lion

Ekisaamunyu
Black Ant

Ekihuguhugu kiine amabara marungi

The butterfly has beautiful colours

Ninkunda kurya enshwa

I like to eat white ants

Nintiina ekinyabwooya

I fear the hairy caterpillar

Enyogori nizishangwa omu myanya ey'oburofa

Maggots are found in dirty places

Orutangura rwine amaguru munana

A spiders has 8 legs

Enda z'omwishokye nizinyeyaguza omutwe

Head lice in the hair make my scalp itchy

Enjoki nizikora obwoki kuruga omu bimuri

Bees make honey from flowers

Enseenene zinuzire munonga

Grass hopers are very delicious

Ebihuguhugu nibizaara amahuri gabyo aha mababi g'ebimuri

Butterflies lay their eggs on the leaves of flowers

Ensiri nizirwaza omushwija gwa *malaria*

Mosquitoes cause malaria fever

Song: Nyamwari

This is a song we sang when playing outside and we came across the small pits/holes in the sand which the baby antlions made to trap small insects for food. As we slowly chipped away the sand to revel the antlions, we sang this song.

We were always fascinated by these creatures because they seemed to move in spasms and backwards as if in a dance to our song. So, we normally danced along as we watched and played with them.

Nyamwari
Nyamwari
Yiguria abaana bataahe
Waba Otarenda ekikooko kyabarya

Nyamwari
Nyamwari
Open for the children to come home
If you don't want the animal will eat them

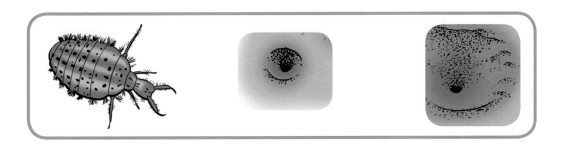

Ebinyonyi
Birds

Enkoko
Chicken

Eshaaki
Rooster

Eihuri
Egg

Embatta
Duck

Ekihungu/Empungu
Eagle

Senkoko
Turkey

Enkombe
Dove

Kasuku
African Grey Parrot

kankomangwa
Woodpecker

Enyonyi
Bird

Ekyashuri
A Birds Nest

Oruyongoyongo
A Heron

Enkyakaara
Guinea Fowl

Endahi
Quail

Entuuha
Crested Crane

Ebendera ya Uganda eine entuuha ahagati yaayo

The Ugandan flag has a crested crane in the center

Eki kyaashuri kirimu amahuri

This nest has eggs in it

Enkoko yéshaki neekokoza omukasheshe ... kookokoriiko....

The rooster crows in the morning...coc- a doole-dooo...

Niturya sekoko buri kyamushana ya sekuukuru

We eat Turkey every Christmas lunch

Amahuri g'endahi nimakye munonga

Qauil eggs are very small

Ekihungu kiriire abukoko bwa shwenkuru bushatu

The eagle ate 3 of grandfather's chicks

Kanyanyazi kaitu nikagarukamu eki orikugamba nka kasuku

Our little sister repeats what you say like a kasuku

Embaata nizikunda kuzaanira omu maizi

Ducks like to play in water

Ebinono by'ekihungu bishongweire

The eagle's claws are very sharp

Oruyongoyongo nirurya obujoka

A heron eats small snakes

Song: Kankomangwa

Tukaba Turiisize

Twazanisa obucence

Obwangye bwanyebayo

Nagarukayo Kubwenda

Nashangayo kankomamgwa

Yanta omukishaho naponga

Sirio Kankomangwa

Sirio Rosebello

We were grazing animals

We played with straws/sticks

I forgot mine behind

So I went back to get them

I found there a woodpecker

He put me in the basket and I was proud

Sirio Woodpecker

Sirio Rosebello

Repeat the song as you dance and at the last line, replace the name with someone else in the game who is picked on

Rhyme: Oruyongoyongo

Oruyongoyongo, orwa Kabare

Orwaisire ente enumi ikaraara

Ekyara kyente kinuza amaizi

Aishi ekintu kyancwa omugongo

Aishi ekintu kyancwa omugongo

Aishi ekintu kyancwa amanyanya

Ente
Cow

Entambura
Transport

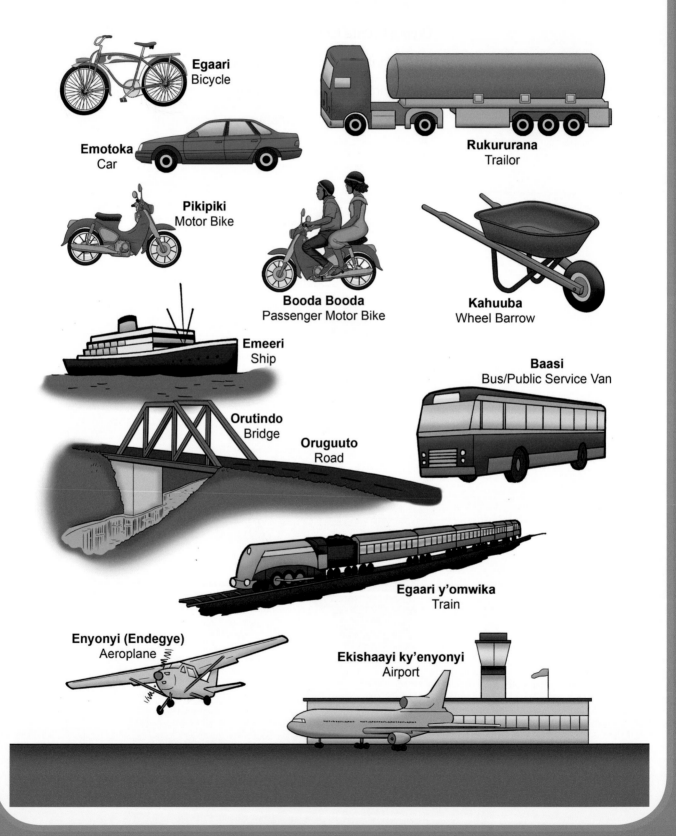

Egaari
Bicycle

Emotoka
Car

Rukururana
Trailor

Pikipiki
Motor Bike

Booda Booda
Passenger Motor Bike

Kahuuba
Wheel Barrow

Emeeri
Ship

Baasi
Bus/Public Service Van

Orutindo
Bridge

Oruguuto
Road

Egaari y'omwika
Train

Enyonyi (Endegye)
Aeroplane

Ekishaayi ky'enyonyi
Airport

Nintiina kukozesa za boda boda

I fear using boda bodas

Egaari y'omwika neetwara abantu bingi munonga

A train can transport many people

Tindikwikirizibwa kuvuga emotoka

I am not allowed to drive a car

Rukururana nizitambura mpoora mpoora

Trailers move very slowly

Enyonyi/endegye nizitambura na sipiidi yamaani

Aeroplanes are fast

Ningyenda ahaishomero na baasi

I go to school by bus

Tindikumanya kwoga

I do not know how to swim

Ninkyega kwoga

I am still learning how to swim

Tinkazaga aha meeri empango

I have never been on a big ship

Ninyambuka orutindo rwahamugyera kuza kutaayaayira nyakwento owa Butembe

I cross the bridge over the river to go to visit my aunt in Butembe

Ninyega kuvuga piki piki

I am learning to drive a motorbike

Okuvuga egaari omuri Holland kyorobi

It is easy to ride a bicycle in Holland

Egaari ya taata ehendekire

My father's bicycle is broken

Makanika w'emotooka nashaba esente nyingi

The car mechanic charges a lot of money

Rhyme

Kanyamunyu

Kanyamunyu okwe nooza hi?

Ninza Igara

Kwendayo enki?

Kurya oburo

Kuburiisa ki?

Kashwigiri

Waaraba hi?

N'omukatookye

Kaahi katookye?

Ka shwenkuru

Waitamu enki?

Nakajoka

Wakaitisa ki?

Kyara kyangye rupimpiri rwamasaka rwita engoma

Kaaguruka kati vivivivivivi

Ebijwaro
Clothes

Kabuuti
Heavy Coat/Rain Coat
(Long Coat)

Eshweta
Sweater

Esaati
Shirt

Ekooti
Coat

Etaayi
Neck Tie

Enkofiira
Hat/Cap

Ekiteteeyi
Dress

Empare
Shorts/Trousers

Engaito
Shoes

Sapato
Sandals/
Slippers

Rugabire
Rubber Sandals

Ekabada
Cupboard

Enkoni
(Walking)
Stick

Empeta
Ring (or Finger)

Orukwanzi
Necklace (Made of Beads)

Enshaho
Bag

Ningorora amasaati n'empaare zangye buri wiki

I iron my shirts and shorts every week

Jwara eshweta yaawe. Hariho embeho

Wear your sweater. It is cold

Oteebwa ekooti/kabuuti yaawe, enjura neeza kugwa nyenkyakare

Don't forget your coat, it will rain tomorrow

Ninkunda kujwara empare engufu omu mushana

I like to wear shorts when its sunny

Engaito za taata nimpango saizi 46

Daddy's shoes are big size 46

Engaito zangye zeishomero zitagukire,

My school shoes are torn

Ninyetaaga engaito ensya

I need new shoes

Ntungire ekiteeteeyi kisya aha mazaarwa gangye

I got a new dress for my birthday

Ekabada eijwire emyenda, engaito n'enshaho

The cupboard is full of clothes, shoes and bags

Enkoni ya shwenkuru yaabura

Grandfather's walking stick is lost

Oije Ondarire

Come for a sleepover

This is a song the Bakiga sing in one of the traditional dances of Ekitaguriro/Ekizino. Can you identify the days of the week and what they plan to do in those days?

Oije Ondaarire x 2

Oije ondaarire orwakatano

Orwamukaaga nsiibe naiwe

Sunday no kushoma yaiwe

Oije ondaarire.

> Come for a sleepover x 2
>
> Come for sleep over on Friday
>
> We spend time together on Saturday
>
> Sunday is the prayer service
>
> Come for a sleepover

Days of the week

Monday - Orwokubanza

Tuesday - Orwakabiri

Wednesday - Orwakashatu

Thursday - Orwakana

Friday - Orwakataano

Saturday - Orwamukaaga

Sunday - Sabiiti/Sande

Emyezi Y'Omwaka
Months of the year

Month of the year	Old way of naming months	New/ commonly used naming
January	Biruuru	Okwokubanza
February	Katambuga	Okwakabiri
March	Kaatumba	Okwakashatu
April	Nyaikoma	Okwakana
May	Kyabahezi	Okwakataano
June	Kahingo	Okwamukaaga
July	Nyairurwe	Okwamushanju
August	Kicuransi/Nyakanga	Okwamunaana
September	Kamena	Okwamwnda
October	Kashwa	Okwikumi
November	Museenene	Okwikumi na Kumwe
December	Muzimbeezi	Okwkumi naibiri

Okubara Eshaaha

Telling time

In the Western world, there is a twenty four hour clock. However, in the Runyankore - Rukiga, telling time, the clock starts at 6 am (marking daylight) so noon would be 6 o'clock and evening similarly starts at 6pm, so 9pm would be 3 o'clock.

12:00am (00:00)
Shaaha Mukaaga Z'eitumbi

12:00pm (12:00)
Shaaha Mukaaga Z'eihangwe

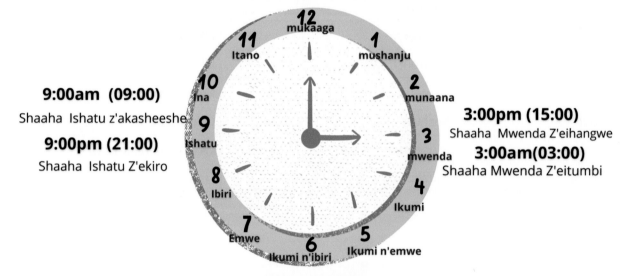

9:00am (09:00)
Shaaha Ishatu z'akasheeshe

9:00pm (21:00)
Shaaha Ishatu Z'ekiro

3:00pm (15:00)
Shaaha Mwenda Z'eihangwe

3:00am(03:00)
Shaaha Mwenda Z'eitumbi

6:00am (06:00)
Shaaha Ikumi n'ibiri Z'akasheeshe

6:00pm (18:00)
Shaaha Ikumi n'ibiri Z'omwazyo

Eriizoba

Today

Hati

Now

Mukasheeshe (AM- Za akasheeshe)

Morning

Eihangwe

Afternoon

Omwebazyo, omumwebazyo

Evening, in the evening

Nyekiro, omukiro

Night, in the night

Bwanyima /Handihakye

Later, afterwards

Nyenkyakare/ Nyensyakare

Tomorrow

Nyomwebazyo

Yesterday

Ijo

The day before yesterday

Butoosha/Buriijo

Always

Obutwire

Forever

Rhyme
Ruhondeza

Omushi.... Omushaija Ruhondeeza

Akabya ....Akabyama ebiro bina

Abyesi ..... Abyesire ekiro kimwe

Ruhonde.... Ruhondeeza mwene Busaasi

The man Ruhondeeza

Slept for 4 days

Thinking it was one day

Ruhondeeza son of Busaasi

Five Senses

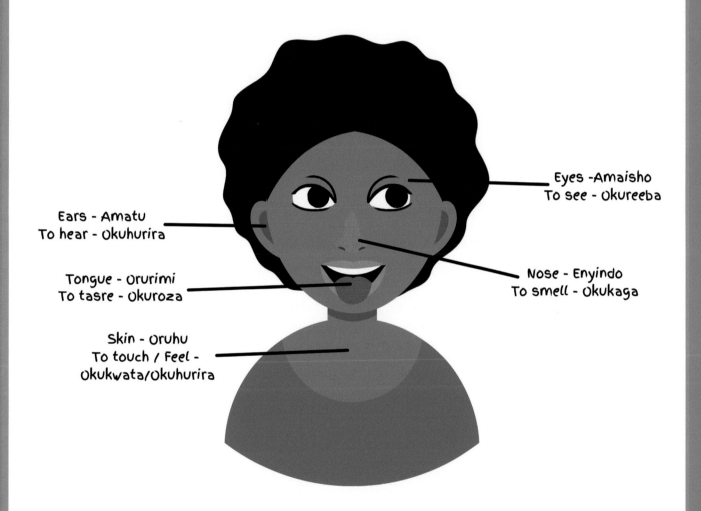

Eyes -Amaisho
To see - Okureeba

Ears - Amatu
To hear - Okuhurira

Nose - Enyindo
To smell - Okukaga

Tongue - Orurimi
To tasre - Okuroza

Skin - Oruhu
To touch / Feel -
Okukwata/Okuhurira

Song: Omutwe amabega amaju ne ebyara

Head shoulders knees and toes

Now you can sing this favourite song in Runyankore.

Omutwe, amabega, amaju ne ebyara, amaju ne ebyara x2

Head, shoulders knees and toes, knees and toes X2

Amaisho, amatu, akanwa n'enyindo

Eyes and ears and mouth and nose

Omutwe, amabega, amaju ne ebyara.

Head, shoulders knees and toes.

More books by the same author from the Mother Tongue Series
Wapwony Acoli- Lets learn Acoli

This book introduces the children to learning the Acoli language by using common items in everyday scenarios that they are likely to encounter. I hope that it will stimulate parents to use in their interactions with children as they learn this exciting new language. The word "pwonya" means teach me. It expresses a desire to learn, and every student needs a teacher. Wapwony Acoli: Let's Learn Acoli is the first of the mother tongue series of books and resources to facilitate the learning of some mother tongue languages of interest

This book shares some of the writer's favourite African sayings. Each chapter contains a category of sayings with a common moral theme, and each theme is meant to teach certain lessons, which include love, patience, unity, discipline, courage, kindness, responsibility, focus, and expected social behaviour or norms. Mollynn shares a mix of scenarios from the past and present to make the content relevant for today's child.

So Said Grandma-Timeless Wisdom from African Sayings

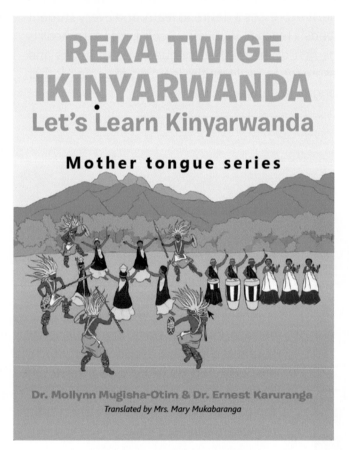

**Reka Twige Ikinyarwanada:
Let's learn Kinyarwanda**

This book introduces one to learning the Kinyarwanda language. It introduces one to common items and phrases in scenarios they are likely to encounter in their daily life. It is meant as a tool for young children and people who want to have an initial introduction to Kinyarwanda. We hope it will stimulate parents to use it in their interactions with children to connect with their Rwandese heritage.

Reka Twige Ikinyarwanda is the third of the mother tongue series of books and resources to facilitate the learning of some mother tongue languages of interest

Printed in the United States
by Baker & Taylor Publisher Services